50 Chocolate Drink Recipes for Home

By: Kelly Johnson

Table of Contents

- Classic Hot Chocolate
- Belgian Hot Chocolate
- Mexican Hot Chocolate
- Spiced Hot Chocolate
- White Hot Chocolate
- Dark Chocolate Hot Chocolate
- Nutella Hot Chocolate
- Raspberry Hot Chocolate
- Mint Hot Chocolate
- Salted Caramel Hot Chocolate
- Peanut Butter Hot Chocolate
- Coconut Hot Chocolate
- Orange Hot Chocolate
- Hazelnut Hot Chocolate
- Almond Hot Chocolate
- Lavender Hot Chocolate
- Cardamom Hot Chocolate
- Chili Hot Chocolate
- Mocha Hot Chocolate
- Irish Hot Chocolate
- Red Velvet Hot Chocolate
- Matcha White Hot Chocolate
- Honey Hot Chocolate
- Maple Hot Chocolate
- Espresso Hot Chocolate
- Cherry Hot Chocolate
- Marshmallow Hot Chocolate
- Pumpkin Spice Hot Chocolate
- Gingerbread Hot Chocolate
- Cookies and Cream Hot Chocolate
- Chocolate Banana Smoothie
- Chocolate Peanut Butter Smoothie
- Chocolate Raspberry Smoothie
- Chocolate Mint Smoothie
- Chocolate Avocado Smoothie

- Chocolate Coconut Smoothie
- Chocolate Strawberry Smoothie
- Chocolate Cherry Smoothie
- Chocolate Almond Smoothie
- Chocolate Oatmeal Smoothie
- Chocolate Chia Seed Pudding
- Chocolate Banana Milkshake
- Chocolate Orange Milkshake
- Chocolate Coffee Milkshake
- Chocolate Caramel Milkshake
- Chocolate Hazelnut Milkshake
- Chocolate Mint Milkshake
- Chocolate Coconut Milkshake
- Chocolate Berry Milkshake
- Chocolate Vanilla Milkshake

Classic Hot Chocolate

Ingredients:

- 2 cups of milk
- 1/4 cup of cocoa powder
- 1/4 cup of granulated sugar
- 1/4 teaspoon of vanilla extract
- Pinch of salt
- Whipped cream or marshmallows (optional, for topping)

Instructions:

1. In a small saucepan, heat the milk over medium heat until it's warm but not boiling.
2. In a separate bowl, mix the cocoa powder, sugar, and salt until well combined.
3. Gradually whisk the cocoa mixture into the warm milk, stirring constantly until it's smooth and well combined.
4. Continue heating the hot chocolate until it's heated through, but be careful not to let it boil.
5. Remove the saucepan from the heat and stir in the vanilla extract.
6. Pour the hot chocolate into mugs and top with whipped cream or marshmallows if desired.
7. Serve hot and enjoy your classic hot chocolate!

Belgian Hot Chocolate

Ingredients:

- 2 cups whole milk
- 1/2 cup heavy cream
- 1/2 cup good quality Belgian dark chocolate, finely chopped
- 2 tablespoons granulated sugar (adjust to taste)
- 1/4 teaspoon vanilla extract
- Pinch of salt
- Whipped cream or chocolate shavings for garnish (optional)

Instructions:

1. In a saucepan, combine the whole milk and heavy cream. Heat over medium-low heat until it starts to simmer, but do not boil.
2. Reduce the heat to low and add the chopped Belgian dark chocolate to the saucepan. Whisk continuously until the chocolate is completely melted and the mixture is smooth.
3. Stir in the granulated sugar, vanilla extract, and a pinch of salt. Taste and adjust the sweetness if needed.
4. Continue to heat the mixture, stirring occasionally, until it's hot and steamy. Be careful not to let it boil.
5. Once heated through, remove the saucepan from the heat and ladle the Belgian hot chocolate into mugs.
6. If desired, top with whipped cream or chocolate shavings for an extra indulgent touch.
7. Serve immediately and enjoy your luxurious Belgian hot chocolate!

Mexican Hot Chocolate

Ingredients:

- 2 cups whole milk
- 2 ounces Mexican chocolate, chopped (such as Ibarra or Abuelita)
- 2 tablespoons unsweetened cocoa powder
- 2 tablespoons granulated sugar (adjust to taste)
- 1/2 teaspoon ground cinnamon
- 1/4 teaspoon ground nutmeg
- Pinch of cayenne pepper (optional, for heat)
- Pinch of salt
- Whipped cream or cinnamon sticks for garnish (optional)

Instructions:

1. In a saucepan, heat the whole milk over medium-low heat until it begins to simmer, but do not boil.
2. Add the chopped Mexican chocolate to the saucepan and whisk until it's completely melted and incorporated into the milk.
3. Whisk in the unsweetened cocoa powder, granulated sugar, ground cinnamon, ground nutmeg, cayenne pepper (if using), and a pinch of salt.
4. Continue to heat the mixture, stirring occasionally, until it's hot and all ingredients are well combined.
5. Taste and adjust the sweetness and spiciness according to your preference by adding more sugar or cayenne pepper if desired.
6. Once heated through and well mixed, remove the saucepan from the heat.
7. Pour the Mexican hot chocolate into mugs and garnish with whipped cream or cinnamon sticks if desired.
8. Serve immediately and enjoy the warming flavors of Mexican hot chocolate!

Spiced Hot Chocolate

Ingredients:

- 2 cups whole milk
- 1/4 cup cocoa powder
- 1/4 cup granulated sugar
- 3 ounces dark chocolate, chopped
- 1/2 teaspoon ground cinnamon
- 1/4 teaspoon ground nutmeg
- 1/8 teaspoon ground cloves
- Pinch of cayenne pepper (adjust to taste)
- Pinch of salt
- Whipped cream or cinnamon sticks for garnish (optional)

Instructions:

1. In a saucepan, heat the whole milk over medium-low heat until it's warm but not boiling.
2. In a separate bowl, mix together the cocoa powder, granulated sugar, ground cinnamon, ground nutmeg, ground cloves, cayenne pepper, and a pinch of salt until well combined.
3. Gradually whisk the cocoa mixture into the warm milk, stirring constantly until it's smooth and well combined.
4. Add the chopped dark chocolate to the saucepan and continue to heat, stirring occasionally, until the chocolate is melted and the mixture is hot.
5. Taste the spiced hot chocolate and adjust the sweetness and spiciness according to your preference by adding more sugar or cayenne pepper if desired.
6. Once heated through and well mixed, remove the saucepan from the heat.
7. Pour the spiced hot chocolate into mugs and garnish with whipped cream or cinnamon sticks if desired.
8. Serve immediately and savor the comforting flavors of spiced hot chocolate!

White Hot Chocolate

Ingredients:

- 2 cups whole milk
- 1 cup heavy cream
- 8 ounces white chocolate, chopped
- 1 teaspoon vanilla extract
- Pinch of salt
- Whipped cream, white chocolate shavings, or sprinkles for garnish (optional)

Instructions:

1. In a saucepan, combine the whole milk and heavy cream. Heat over medium-low heat until it's warm but not boiling.
2. Add the chopped white chocolate to the saucepan and stir until it's completely melted and the mixture is smooth.
3. Stir in the vanilla extract and a pinch of salt, mixing until well combined.
4. Continue to heat the white hot chocolate, stirring occasionally, until it's hot and steamy. Be careful not to let it boil.
5. Once heated through, remove the saucepan from the heat.
6. Pour the white hot chocolate into mugs and garnish with whipped cream, white chocolate shavings, or sprinkles if desired.
7. Serve immediately and enjoy the luxurious creaminess of white hot chocolate!

Dark Chocolate Hot Chocolate

Ingredients:

- 2 cups whole milk
- 1/2 cup heavy cream
- 6 ounces dark chocolate (at least 70% cocoa), finely chopped
- 2 tablespoons granulated sugar (adjust to taste)
- 1/2 teaspoon vanilla extract
- Pinch of salt
- Whipped cream or dark chocolate shavings for garnish (optional)

Instructions:

1. In a saucepan, combine the whole milk and heavy cream. Heat over medium-low heat until it's warm but not boiling.
2. Add the finely chopped dark chocolate to the saucepan and stir until it's completely melted and the mixture is smooth.
3. Stir in the granulated sugar, vanilla extract, and a pinch of salt, mixing until well combined. Taste and adjust the sweetness if needed.
4. Continue to heat the dark chocolate hot chocolate, stirring occasionally, until it's hot and steamy. Be careful not to let it boil.
5. Once heated through, remove the saucepan from the heat.
6. Pour the dark chocolate hot chocolate into mugs and garnish with whipped cream or dark chocolate shavings if desired.
7. Serve immediately and indulge in the rich flavors of dark chocolate hot chocolate!

Nutella Hot Chocolate

Ingredients:

- 2 cups milk (whole or any milk of your choice)
- 1/4 cup Nutella
- 2 tablespoons cocoa powder
- 2 tablespoons granulated sugar (adjust to taste)
- Optional toppings: whipped cream, marshmallows, chocolate syrup, or Nutella drizzle

Instructions:

1. In a small saucepan, heat the milk over medium-low heat until it's warm but not boiling.
2. Add Nutella to the saucepan and whisk until it's completely melted and incorporated into the milk.
3. Whisk in the cocoa powder and granulated sugar until well combined.
4. Continue to heat the mixture, stirring occasionally, until it's hot and steamy. Be careful not to let it boil.
5. Once heated through and well mixed, remove the saucepan from the heat.
6. Pour the Nutella hot chocolate into mugs.
7. If desired, top with whipped cream, marshmallows, chocolate syrup, or a drizzle of Nutella.
8. Serve immediately and enjoy the creamy and chocolatey goodness of Nutella hot chocolate!

Raspberry Hot Chocolate

Ingredients:

- 2 cups milk (whole or any milk of your choice)
- 1/4 cup raspberry puree (made by blending fresh or thawed frozen raspberries)
- 2 tablespoons cocoa powder
- 2 tablespoons granulated sugar (adjust to taste)
- 1/4 teaspoon vanilla extract
- Optional toppings: whipped cream, fresh raspberries, chocolate shavings

Instructions:

1. In a small saucepan, heat the milk over medium-low heat until it's warm but not boiling.
2. Add the raspberry puree to the saucepan and whisk until it's well incorporated into the milk.
3. Whisk in the cocoa powder and granulated sugar until fully dissolved and the mixture is smooth.
4. Add the vanilla extract and stir until combined.
5. Continue to heat the raspberry hot chocolate, stirring occasionally, until it's hot and steamy. Be careful not to let it boil.
6. Once heated through, remove the saucepan from the heat.
7. Pour the raspberry hot chocolate into mugs.
8. If desired, top with whipped cream, fresh raspberries, or chocolate shavings.
9. Serve immediately and enjoy the delightful combination of raspberry and chocolate flavors in this cozy beverage!

Mint Hot Chocolate

Ingredients:

- 2 cups milk (whole or any milk of your choice)
- 1/4 teaspoon peppermint extract
- 2 tablespoons cocoa powder
- 2 tablespoons granulated sugar (adjust to taste)
- Optional toppings: whipped cream, chocolate shavings, mint leaves

Instructions:

1. In a small saucepan, heat the milk over medium-low heat until it's warm but not boiling.
2. Stir in the cocoa powder and granulated sugar until fully dissolved and the mixture is smooth.
3. Add the peppermint extract to the saucepan and stir until well combined.
4. Continue to heat the mint hot chocolate, stirring occasionally, until it's hot and steamy. Be careful not to let it boil.
5. Once heated through, remove the saucepan from the heat.
6. Pour the mint hot chocolate into mugs.
7. If desired, top with whipped cream, chocolate shavings, or mint leaves for garnish.
8. Serve immediately and enjoy the cool, refreshing flavor of mint combined with rich chocolate!

Salted Caramel Hot Chocolate

Ingredients:

- 2 cups milk (whole or any milk of your choice)
- 2 tablespoons cocoa powder
- 2 tablespoons granulated sugar (adjust to taste)
- 2 tablespoons caramel sauce (plus extra for drizzling)
- 1/4 teaspoon vanilla extract
- Pinch of salt
- Optional toppings: whipped cream, caramel sauce, sea salt flakes

Instructions:

1. In a small saucepan, heat the milk over medium-low heat until it's warm but not boiling.
2. Stir in the cocoa powder and granulated sugar until fully dissolved and the mixture is smooth.
3. Add the caramel sauce and vanilla extract to the saucepan, stirring until well combined.
4. Add a pinch of salt to enhance the flavor and stir again.
5. Continue to heat the salted caramel hot chocolate, stirring occasionally, until it's hot and steamy. Be careful not to let it boil.
6. Once heated through, remove the saucepan from the heat.
7. Pour the salted caramel hot chocolate into mugs.
8. If desired, top with whipped cream and drizzle extra caramel sauce on top.
9. Sprinkle a few sea salt flakes over the whipped cream for a delightful contrast of flavors.
10. Serve immediately and enjoy the perfect balance of sweet caramel and a touch of saltiness in this comforting beverage!

Peanut Butter Hot Chocolate

Ingredients:

- 2 cups milk (whole or any milk of your choice)
- 2 tablespoons cocoa powder
- 2 tablespoons granulated sugar (adjust to taste)
- 2 tablespoons creamy peanut butter
- 1/4 teaspoon vanilla extract
- Optional toppings: whipped cream, chocolate shavings, crushed peanuts

Instructions:

1. In a small saucepan, heat the milk over medium-low heat until it's warm but not boiling.
2. Stir in the cocoa powder and granulated sugar until fully dissolved and the mixture is smooth.
3. Add the creamy peanut butter to the saucepan, stirring until it's completely melted and incorporated into the milk.
4. Stir in the vanilla extract until well combined.
5. Continue to heat the peanut butter hot chocolate, stirring occasionally, until it's hot and steamy. Be careful not to let it boil.
6. Once heated through, remove the saucepan from the heat.
7. Pour the peanut butter hot chocolate into mugs.
8. If desired, top with whipped cream, chocolate shavings, or crushed peanuts for garnish.
9. Serve immediately and enjoy the creamy and nutty goodness of peanut butter combined with rich chocolate!

Coconut Hot Chocolate

Ingredients:

- 2 cups coconut milk (canned or carton)
- 2 tablespoons cocoa powder
- 2 tablespoons granulated sugar (adjust to taste)
- 1/4 cup shredded coconut (sweetened or unsweetened)
- 1/4 teaspoon vanilla extract
- Optional toppings: whipped cream, toasted coconut flakes, chocolate shavings

Instructions:

1. In a small saucepan, heat the coconut milk over medium-low heat until it's warm but not boiling.
2. Stir in the cocoa powder and granulated sugar until fully dissolved and the mixture is smooth.
3. Add the shredded coconut to the saucepan, stirring occasionally, and let it simmer for about 5 minutes to infuse the coconut flavor.
4. Stir in the vanilla extract until well combined.
5. Continue to heat the coconut hot chocolate, stirring occasionally, until it's hot and steamy. Be careful not to let it boil.
6. Once heated through, remove the saucepan from the heat.
7. Pour the coconut hot chocolate into mugs.
8. If desired, top with whipped cream, toasted coconut flakes, or chocolate shavings for garnish.
9. Serve immediately and enjoy the tropical twist of coconut combined with rich chocolate!

Orange Hot Chocolate

Ingredients:

- 2 cups milk (whole or any milk of your choice)
- Zest of 1 orange
- 2 tablespoons cocoa powder
- 2 tablespoons granulated sugar (adjust to taste)
- 1/4 teaspoon vanilla extract
- Optional toppings: whipped cream, orange zest curls, chocolate shavings

Instructions:

1. In a small saucepan, heat the milk over medium-low heat until it's warm but not boiling.
2. Add the orange zest to the saucepan and let it simmer for about 5 minutes to infuse the orange flavor into the milk.
3. Remove the orange zest from the milk using a fine-mesh strainer or spoon.
4. Stir in the cocoa powder and granulated sugar until fully dissolved and the mixture is smooth.
5. Add the vanilla extract to the saucepan and stir until well combined.
6. Continue to heat the orange hot chocolate, stirring occasionally, until it's hot and steamy. Be careful not to let it boil.
7. Once heated through, remove the saucepan from the heat.
8. Pour the orange hot chocolate into mugs.
9. If desired, top with whipped cream, orange zest curls, or chocolate shavings for garnish.
10. Serve immediately and enjoy the refreshing citrus flavor of orange combined with rich chocolate!

Hazelnut Hot Chocolate

Ingredients:

- 2 cups milk (whole or any milk of your choice)
- 2 tablespoons cocoa powder
- 2 tablespoons granulated sugar (adjust to taste)
- 2 tablespoons hazelnut spread (such as Nutella)
- 1/4 teaspoon vanilla extract
- Optional toppings: whipped cream, chopped hazelnuts, chocolate shavings

Instructions:

1. In a small saucepan, heat the milk over medium-low heat until it's warm but not boiling.
2. Stir in the cocoa powder and granulated sugar until fully dissolved and the mixture is smooth.
3. Add the hazelnut spread to the saucepan, stirring until it's completely melted and incorporated into the milk.
4. Stir in the vanilla extract until well combined.
5. Continue to heat the hazelnut hot chocolate, stirring occasionally, until it's hot and steamy. Be careful not to let it boil.
6. Once heated through, remove the saucepan from the heat.
7. Pour the hazelnut hot chocolate into mugs.
8. If desired, top with whipped cream, chopped hazelnuts, or chocolate shavings for garnish.
9. Serve immediately and enjoy the rich and nutty flavor of hazelnut combined with indulgent chocolate!

Almond Hot Chocolate

Ingredients:

- 2 cups milk (whole or any milk of your choice)
- 2 tablespoons cocoa powder
- 2 tablespoons granulated sugar (adjust to taste)
- 1/4 teaspoon almond extract
- Optional toppings: whipped cream, sliced almonds, chocolate shavings

Instructions:

1. In a small saucepan, heat the milk over medium-low heat until it's warm but not boiling.
2. Stir in the cocoa powder and granulated sugar until fully dissolved and the mixture is smooth.
3. Add the almond extract to the saucepan and stir until well combined.
4. Continue to heat the almond hot chocolate, stirring occasionally, until it's hot and steamy. Be careful not to let it boil.
5. Once heated through, remove the saucepan from the heat.
6. Pour the almond hot chocolate into mugs.
7. If desired, top with whipped cream, sliced almonds, or chocolate shavings for garnish.
8. Serve immediately and enjoy the comforting flavor of almond combined with rich chocolate!

Lavender Hot Chocolate

Ingredients:

- 2 cups milk (whole or any milk of your choice)
- 2 tablespoons cocoa powder
- 2 tablespoons granulated sugar (adjust to taste)
- 1 teaspoon culinary lavender buds (dried)
- Optional toppings: whipped cream, lavender flowers for garnish

Instructions:

1. In a small saucepan, heat the milk over medium-low heat until it's warm but not boiling.
2. Add the culinary lavender buds to the saucepan and let them steep in the warm milk for about 5 minutes to infuse the lavender flavor.
3. Strain the lavender-infused milk using a fine-mesh strainer or cheesecloth to remove the lavender buds.
4. Return the infused milk to the saucepan and discard the lavender buds.
5. Stir in the cocoa powder and granulated sugar until fully dissolved and the mixture is smooth.
6. Continue to heat the lavender hot chocolate, stirring occasionally, until it's hot and steamy. Be careful not to let it boil.
7. Once heated through, remove the saucepan from the heat.
8. Pour the lavender hot chocolate into mugs.
9. If desired, top with whipped cream and garnish with a few lavender flowers for a decorative touch.
10. Serve immediately and enjoy the soothing and fragrant flavor of lavender combined with rich chocolate!

Cardamom Hot Chocolate

Ingredients:

- 2 cups milk (whole or any milk of your choice)
- 2 tablespoons cocoa powder
- 2 tablespoons granulated sugar (adjust to taste)
- 1/4 teaspoon ground cardamom
- Pinch of ground cinnamon (optional)
- Pinch of ground nutmeg (optional)
- Optional toppings: whipped cream, chocolate shavings, ground cardamom for garnish

Instructions:

1. In a small saucepan, heat the milk over medium-low heat until it's warm but not boiling.
2. Stir in the cocoa powder and granulated sugar until fully dissolved and the mixture is smooth.
3. Add the ground cardamom to the saucepan and stir until well combined.
4. Optionally, add a pinch of ground cinnamon and ground nutmeg for additional flavor.
5. Continue to heat the cardamom hot chocolate, stirring occasionally, until it's hot and steamy. Be careful not to let it boil.
6. Once heated through, remove the saucepan from the heat.
7. Pour the cardamom hot chocolate into mugs.
8. If desired, top with whipped cream and garnish with a sprinkle of ground cardamom or chocolate shavings.
9. Serve immediately and enjoy the exotic and aromatic flavor of cardamom combined with rich chocolate!

Chili Hot Chocolate

Ingredients:

- 2 cups milk (whole or any milk of your choice)
- 2 tablespoons cocoa powder
- 2 tablespoons granulated sugar (adjust to taste)
- 1/4 teaspoon ground cinnamon
- Pinch of chili powder or cayenne pepper (adjust to taste)
- Pinch of salt
- Optional toppings: whipped cream, chili powder/cayenne pepper for garnish, cinnamon stick for stirring

Instructions:

1. In a small saucepan, heat the milk over medium-low heat until it's warm but not boiling.
2. Stir in the cocoa powder and granulated sugar until fully dissolved and the mixture is smooth.
3. Add the ground cinnamon, a pinch of chili powder or cayenne pepper, and a pinch of salt to the saucepan.
4. Stir well to combine all the ingredients.
5. Taste the mixture and adjust the sweetness and spiciness according to your preference by adding more sugar or chili powder/cayenne pepper if needed.
6. Continue to heat the chili hot chocolate, stirring occasionally, until it's hot and steamy. Be careful not to let it boil.
7. Once heated through, remove the saucepan from the heat.
8. Pour the chili hot chocolate into mugs.
9. If desired, top with whipped cream and garnish with a sprinkle of chili powder or cayenne pepper for an extra kick.
10. Serve immediately with a cinnamon stick for stirring, and enjoy the spicy warmth of chili combined with rich chocolate!

Mocha Hot Chocolate

Ingredients:

- 2 cups milk (whole or any milk of your choice)
- 2 tablespoons cocoa powder
- 2 tablespoons granulated sugar (adjust to taste)
- 2 shots of espresso (or 1/2 cup strong brewed coffee)
- Optional toppings: whipped cream, chocolate shavings, cocoa powder for garnish

Instructions:

1. In a small saucepan, heat the milk over medium-low heat until it's warm but not boiling.
2. Stir in the cocoa powder and granulated sugar until fully dissolved and the mixture is smooth.
3. Brew the espresso or strong coffee separately.
4. Once the milk mixture is hot, stir in the brewed espresso or coffee.
5. Continue to heat the mocha hot chocolate, stirring occasionally, until it's hot and steamy. Be careful not to let it boil.
6. Once heated through, remove the saucepan from the heat.
7. Pour the mocha hot chocolate into mugs.
8. If desired, top with whipped cream and garnish with chocolate shavings or a sprinkle of cocoa powder.
9. Serve immediately and enjoy the rich and indulgent flavor of mocha combined with chocolate!

Irish Hot Chocolate

Ingredients:

- 2 cups milk (whole or any milk of your choice)
- 2 tablespoons cocoa powder
- 2 tablespoons granulated sugar (adjust to taste)
- 2 ounces Irish cream liqueur (such as Baileys)
- Optional toppings: whipped cream, chocolate shavings, cocoa powder for garnish

Instructions:

1. In a small saucepan, heat the milk over medium-low heat until it's warm but not boiling.
2. Stir in the cocoa powder and granulated sugar until fully dissolved and the mixture is smooth.
3. Once the milk mixture is hot, stir in the Irish cream liqueur.
4. Continue to heat the Irish hot chocolate, stirring occasionally, until it's hot and steamy. Be careful not to let it boil.
5. Once heated through, remove the saucepan from the heat.
6. Pour the Irish hot chocolate into mugs.
7. If desired, top with whipped cream and garnish with chocolate shavings or a sprinkle of cocoa powder.
8. Serve immediately and enjoy the warm and indulgent flavor of Irish hot chocolate!

Red Velvet Hot Chocolate

Ingredients:

- 2 cups milk (whole or any milk of your choice)
- 2 tablespoons cocoa powder
- 2 tablespoons granulated sugar (adjust to taste)
- 1 teaspoon vanilla extract
- 1/4 teaspoon red food coloring
- Optional toppings: whipped cream, chocolate shavings, red velvet cake crumbs

Instructions:

1. In a small saucepan, heat the milk over medium-low heat until it's warm but not boiling.
2. Stir in the cocoa powder and granulated sugar until fully dissolved and the mixture is smooth.
3. Add the vanilla extract to the saucepan and stir until well combined.
4. Add the red food coloring to the saucepan, stirring until the hot chocolate turns red and is evenly colored.
5. Continue to heat the red velvet hot chocolate, stirring occasionally, until it's hot and steamy. Be careful not to let it boil.
6. Once heated through, remove the saucepan from the heat.
7. Pour the red velvet hot chocolate into mugs.
8. If desired, top with whipped cream and garnish with chocolate shavings or red velvet cake crumbs.
9. Serve immediately and enjoy the rich and vibrant flavor of red velvet hot chocolate!

Matcha White Hot Chocolate

Ingredients:

- 2 cups milk (whole or any milk of your choice)
- 1 tablespoon matcha powder
- 1/4 cup white chocolate chips or chopped white chocolate
- 2 tablespoons granulated sugar (adjust to taste)
- 1/4 teaspoon vanilla extract
- Optional toppings: whipped cream, matcha powder for dusting

Instructions:

1. In a small saucepan, heat the milk over medium-low heat until it's warm but not boiling.
2. In a separate bowl, whisk together the matcha powder and granulated sugar until well combined.
3. Gradually whisk the matcha mixture into the warm milk, stirring constantly until it's fully incorporated and smooth.
4. Add the white chocolate chips or chopped white chocolate to the saucepan and stir until melted and the mixture is smooth.
5. Stir in the vanilla extract until well combined.
6. Continue to heat the matcha white hot chocolate, stirring occasionally, until it's hot and steamy. Be careful not to let it boil.
7. Once heated through, remove the saucepan from the heat.
8. Pour the matcha white hot chocolate into mugs.
9. If desired, top with whipped cream and dust with a sprinkle of matcha powder for garnish.
10. Serve immediately and enjoy the unique and delightful flavor of matcha combined with creamy white chocolate!

Honey Hot Chocolate

Ingredients:

- 2 cups milk (whole or any milk of your choice)
- 2 tablespoons cocoa powder
- 2 tablespoons honey (adjust to taste)
- 1/4 teaspoon vanilla extract
- Pinch of salt
- Optional toppings: whipped cream, chocolate shavings, drizzle of honey

Instructions:

1. In a small saucepan, heat the milk over medium-low heat until it's warm but not boiling.
2. Stir in the cocoa powder and honey until fully dissolved and the mixture is smooth.
3. Add the vanilla extract and a pinch of salt to the saucepan, stirring until well combined.
4. Continue to heat the honey hot chocolate, stirring occasionally, until it's hot and steamy. Be careful not to let it boil.
5. Once heated through, remove the saucepan from the heat.
6. Pour the honey hot chocolate into mugs.
7. If desired, top with whipped cream, chocolate shavings, and a drizzle of honey for garnish.
8. Serve immediately and enjoy the comforting sweetness of honey combined with rich chocolate!

Maple Hot Chocolate

Ingredients:

- 2 cups milk (whole or any milk of your choice)
- 2 tablespoons cocoa powder
- 2 tablespoons pure maple syrup (adjust to taste)
- 1/4 teaspoon vanilla extract
- Pinch of salt
- Optional toppings: whipped cream, chocolate shavings, drizzle of maple syrup

Instructions:

1. In a small saucepan, heat the milk over medium-low heat until it's warm but not boiling.
2. Stir in the cocoa powder and maple syrup until fully dissolved and the mixture is smooth.
3. Add the vanilla extract and a pinch of salt to the saucepan, stirring until well combined.
4. Continue to heat the maple hot chocolate, stirring occasionally, until it's hot and steamy. Be careful not to let it boil.
5. Once heated through, remove the saucepan from the heat.
6. Pour the maple hot chocolate into mugs.
7. If desired, top with whipped cream, chocolate shavings, and a drizzle of maple syrup for garnish.
8. Serve immediately and enjoy the comforting sweetness of maple combined with rich chocolate!

Espresso Hot Chocolate

Ingredients:

- 2 cups milk (whole or any milk of your choice)
- 2 tablespoons cocoa powder
- 2 tablespoons granulated sugar (adjust to taste)
- 2 shots of espresso (or 1/2 cup strong brewed coffee)
- 1/4 teaspoon vanilla extract
- Optional toppings: whipped cream, chocolate shavings, cocoa powder for garnish

Instructions:

1. In a small saucepan, heat the milk over medium-low heat until it's warm but not boiling.
2. Stir in the cocoa powder and granulated sugar until fully dissolved and the mixture is smooth.
3. Brew the espresso or strong coffee separately.
4. Once the milk mixture is hot, stir in the brewed espresso or coffee.
5. Continue to heat the espresso hot chocolate, stirring occasionally, until it's hot and steamy. Be careful not to let it boil.
6. Once heated through, remove the saucepan from the heat.
7. Stir in the vanilla extract until well combined.
8. Pour the espresso hot chocolate into mugs.
9. If desired, top with whipped cream and garnish with chocolate shavings or a sprinkle of cocoa powder.
10. Serve immediately and enjoy the rich and bold flavor of espresso combined with chocolate!

Cherry Hot Chocolate

Ingredients:

- 2 cups milk (whole or any milk of your choice)
- 2 tablespoons cocoa powder
- 2 tablespoons granulated sugar (adjust to taste)
- 1/4 teaspoon almond extract
- 1/4 cup cherry preserves or cherry syrup
- Optional toppings: whipped cream, chocolate shavings, maraschino cherries

Instructions:

1. In a small saucepan, heat the milk over medium-low heat until it's warm but not boiling.
2. Stir in the cocoa powder and granulated sugar until fully dissolved and the mixture is smooth.
3. Add the almond extract to the saucepan and stir until well combined.
4. Stir in the cherry preserves or cherry syrup until incorporated into the hot chocolate mixture.
5. Continue to heat the cherry hot chocolate, stirring occasionally, until it's hot and steamy. Be careful not to let it boil.
6. Once heated through, remove the saucepan from the heat.
7. Pour the cherry hot chocolate into mugs.
8. If desired, top with whipped cream and garnish with chocolate shavings or a maraschino cherry.
9. Serve immediately and enjoy the delightful combination of cherry flavor with rich chocolate!

Marshmallow Hot Chocolate

Ingredients:

- 2 cups milk (whole or any milk of your choice)
- 2 tablespoons cocoa powder
- 2 tablespoons granulated sugar (adjust to taste)
- Marshmallows (as many as desired)
- Optional toppings: whipped cream, chocolate syrup, chocolate shavings

Instructions:

1. In a small saucepan, heat the milk over medium-low heat until it's warm but not boiling.
2. Stir in the cocoa powder and granulated sugar until fully dissolved and the mixture is smooth.
3. Once the hot chocolate is ready, pour it into mugs.
4. Top each mug with marshmallows.
5. If desired, add a dollop of whipped cream on top of the marshmallows.
6. Optionally, drizzle some chocolate syrup over the whipped cream or sprinkle chocolate shavings.
7. Serve immediately and enjoy the cozy comfort of marshmallow hot chocolate!

Pumpkin Spice Hot Chocolate

Ingredients:

- 2 cups milk (whole or any milk of your choice)
- 2 tablespoons cocoa powder
- 2 tablespoons granulated sugar (adjust to taste)
- 1/4 cup pumpkin puree
- 1/2 teaspoon pumpkin pie spice
- Optional toppings: whipped cream, cinnamon, chocolate shavings

Instructions:

1. In a small saucepan, heat the milk over medium-low heat until it's warm but not boiling.
2. Stir in the cocoa powder and granulated sugar until fully dissolved and the mixture is smooth.
3. Add the pumpkin puree and pumpkin pie spice to the saucepan, stirring until well combined.
4. Continue to heat the pumpkin spice hot chocolate, stirring occasionally, until it's hot and steamy. Be careful not to let it boil.
5. Once heated through, remove the saucepan from the heat.
6. Pour the pumpkin spice hot chocolate into mugs.
7. If desired, top with whipped cream and sprinkle with cinnamon or chocolate shavings.
8. Serve immediately and enjoy the cozy flavors of pumpkin spice combined with rich chocolate!

Gingerbread Hot Chocolate

Ingredients:

- 2 cups milk (whole or any milk of your choice)
- 2 tablespoons cocoa powder
- 2 tablespoons brown sugar (adjust to taste)
- 1/2 teaspoon ground ginger
- 1/4 teaspoon ground cinnamon
- 1/8 teaspoon ground nutmeg
- 1/8 teaspoon ground cloves
- Pinch of salt
- Whipped cream, gingerbread cookie crumbs, or cinnamon sticks for garnish (optional)

Instructions:

1. In a small saucepan, heat the milk over medium-low heat until it's warm but not boiling.
2. Stir in the cocoa powder and brown sugar until fully dissolved and the mixture is smooth.
3. Add the ground ginger, ground cinnamon, ground nutmeg, ground cloves, and a pinch of salt to the saucepan, stirring until well combined.
4. Continue to heat the gingerbread hot chocolate, stirring occasionally, until it's hot and steamy. Be careful not to let it boil.
5. Once heated through, remove the saucepan from the heat.
6. Pour the gingerbread hot chocolate into mugs.
7. If desired, top with whipped cream and sprinkle with gingerbread cookie crumbs or garnish with a cinnamon stick.
8. Serve immediately and enjoy the cozy flavors of gingerbread combined with rich chocolate!

Cookies and Cream Hot Chocolate

Ingredients:

- 2 cups milk (whole or any milk of your choice)
- 2 tablespoons cocoa powder
- 2 tablespoons granulated sugar (adjust to taste)
- 1/4 cup crushed chocolate sandwich cookies (such as Oreo cookies)
- Optional toppings: whipped cream, additional crushed cookies, chocolate syrup

Instructions:

1. In a small saucepan, heat the milk over medium-low heat until it's warm but not boiling.
2. Stir in the cocoa powder and granulated sugar until fully dissolved and the mixture is smooth.
3. Add the crushed chocolate sandwich cookies to the saucepan, stirring until they are incorporated into the hot chocolate mixture.
4. Continue to heat the cookies and cream hot chocolate, stirring occasionally, until it's hot and steamy. Be careful not to let it boil.
5. Once heated through, remove the saucepan from the heat.
6. Pour the cookies and cream hot chocolate into mugs.
7. If desired, top with whipped cream and sprinkle with additional crushed cookies.
8. Optionally, drizzle with chocolate syrup for extra indulgence.
9. Serve immediately and enjoy the delightful combination of cookies and cream with rich chocolate!

Chocolate Banana Smoothie

Ingredients:

- 1 ripe banana
- 1 cup milk (dairy or plant-based)
- 1 tablespoon cocoa powder
- 1 tablespoon honey or maple syrup (optional, adjust to taste)
- 1/2 teaspoon vanilla extract
- Ice cubes (optional, for a colder smoothie)
- Optional add-ins: a handful of spinach or kale, a tablespoon of peanut butter or almond butter, a scoop of protein powder

Instructions:

1. Peel the banana and break it into chunks.
2. In a blender, combine the banana chunks, milk, cocoa powder, honey or maple syrup (if using), and vanilla extract.
3. If desired, add any optional add-ins such as spinach or kale, nut butter, or protein powder.
4. Blend on high speed until smooth and creamy.
5. Taste the smoothie and adjust the sweetness or cocoa intensity if needed by adding more honey, cocoa powder, or vanilla extract.
6. If you prefer a colder smoothie, add a handful of ice cubes and blend again until smooth.
7. Once blended to your desired consistency, pour the chocolate banana smoothie into glasses.
8. Optionally, garnish with a sprinkle of cocoa powder or sliced bananas on top.
9. Serve immediately and enjoy the creamy and chocolaty goodness of this refreshing smoothie!

Chocolate Peanut Butter Smoothie

Ingredients:

- 1 ripe banana
- 1 cup milk (dairy or plant-based)
- 2 tablespoons cocoa powder
- 2 tablespoons peanut butter (creamy or crunchy)
- 1 tablespoon honey or maple syrup (optional, adjust to taste)
- 1/2 teaspoon vanilla extract
- Ice cubes (optional, for a colder smoothie)
- Optional add-ins: a handful of spinach or kale, a scoop of protein powder, a tablespoon of flaxseeds or chia seeds

Instructions:

1. Peel the banana and break it into chunks.
2. In a blender, combine the banana chunks, milk, cocoa powder, peanut butter, honey or maple syrup (if using), and vanilla extract.
3. If desired, add any optional add-ins such as spinach or kale, protein powder, or seeds.
4. Blend on high speed until smooth and creamy.
5. Taste the smoothie and adjust the sweetness or peanut butter intensity if needed by adding more honey, peanut butter, or cocoa powder.
6. If you prefer a colder smoothie, add a handful of ice cubes and blend again until smooth.
7. Once blended to your desired consistency, pour the chocolate peanut butter smoothie into glasses.
8. Optionally, garnish with a drizzle of peanut butter or a sprinkle of cocoa powder on top.
9. Serve immediately and enjoy the creamy and nutty flavor of this indulgent smoothie!

Chocolate Raspberry Smoothie

Ingredients:

- 1 cup frozen raspberries
- 1 ripe banana
- 1 cup milk (dairy or plant-based)
- 2 tablespoons cocoa powder
- 1 tablespoon honey or maple syrup (optional, adjust to taste)
- 1/2 teaspoon vanilla extract
- Ice cubes (optional, for a colder smoothie)
- Optional add-ins: a handful of spinach or kale, a scoop of protein powder, a tablespoon of flaxseeds or chia seeds

Instructions:

1. In a blender, combine the frozen raspberries, banana, milk, cocoa powder, honey or maple syrup (if using), and vanilla extract.
2. If desired, add any optional add-ins such as spinach or kale, protein powder, or seeds.
3. Blend on high speed until smooth and creamy.
4. Taste the smoothie and adjust the sweetness if needed by adding more honey or maple syrup.
5. If you prefer a colder smoothie, add a handful of ice cubes and blend again until smooth.
6. Once blended to your desired consistency, pour the chocolate raspberry smoothie into glasses.
7. Optionally, garnish with a few fresh raspberries or a sprinkle of cocoa powder on top.
8. Serve immediately and enjoy the refreshing and chocolaty flavor of this delightful smoothie!

Chocolate Mint Smoothie

Ingredients:

- 1 ripe banana
- 1 cup milk (dairy or plant-based)
- 2 tablespoons cocoa powder
- 1 tablespoon honey or maple syrup (optional, adjust to taste)
- 1/4 teaspoon peppermint extract (adjust to taste)
- Handful of fresh spinach or kale (optional)
- Ice cubes (optional, for a colder smoothie)
- Optional add-ins: a scoop of protein powder, a tablespoon of chia seeds or flaxseeds

Instructions:

1. In a blender, combine the ripe banana, milk, cocoa powder, honey or maple syrup (if using), and peppermint extract.
2. If desired, add a handful of fresh spinach or kale for added nutrients.
3. Blend the ingredients on high speed until smooth and creamy.
4. Taste the smoothie and adjust the sweetness or mint flavor if needed by adding more honey or maple syrup, or more peppermint extract.
5. If you prefer a colder smoothie, add a handful of ice cubes and blend again until smooth.
6. Once blended to your desired consistency, pour the chocolate mint smoothie into glasses.
7. Serve immediately and enjoy the cool and refreshing taste of chocolate combined with mint!

Chocolate Avocado Smoothie

Ingredients:

- 1 ripe avocado, peeled and pitted
- 1 ripe banana
- 1 cup milk (dairy or plant-based)
- 2 tablespoons cocoa powder
- 1-2 tablespoons honey or maple syrup (adjust to taste)
- 1/2 teaspoon vanilla extract
- Ice cubes (optional, for a colder smoothie)
- Optional add-ins: a handful of spinach or kale, a scoop of protein powder, a tablespoon of chia seeds or flaxseeds

Instructions:

1. In a blender, combine the ripe avocado, banana, milk, cocoa powder, honey or maple syrup, and vanilla extract.
2. If desired, add any optional add-ins such as spinach or kale, protein powder, or seeds.
3. Blend the ingredients on high speed until smooth and creamy.
4. Taste the smoothie and adjust the sweetness if needed by adding more honey or maple syrup.
5. If you prefer a colder smoothie, add a handful of ice cubes and blend again until smooth.
6. Once blended to your desired consistency, pour the chocolate avocado smoothie into glasses.
7. Serve immediately and enjoy the creamy and chocolaty goodness of this nutritious smoothie!

Chocolate Coconut Smoothie

Ingredients:

- 1 ripe banana
- 1 cup coconut milk (canned or carton)
- 2 tablespoons cocoa powder
- 2 tablespoons shredded coconut (sweetened or unsweetened)
- 1-2 tablespoons honey or maple syrup (adjust to taste)
- 1/2 teaspoon vanilla extract
- Ice cubes (optional, for a colder smoothie)
- Optional add-ins: a tablespoon of coconut yogurt, a scoop of protein powder, a tablespoon of chia seeds or flaxseeds

Instructions:

1. In a blender, combine the ripe banana, coconut milk, cocoa powder, shredded coconut, honey or maple syrup, and vanilla extract.
2. If desired, add any optional add-ins such as coconut yogurt, protein powder, or seeds.
3. Blend the ingredients on high speed until smooth and creamy.
4. Taste the smoothie and adjust the sweetness if needed by adding more honey or maple syrup.
5. If you prefer a colder smoothie, add a handful of ice cubes and blend again until smooth.
6. Once blended to your desired consistency, pour the chocolate coconut smoothie into glasses.
7. Serve immediately and enjoy the tropical flavor of coconut combined with rich chocolate!

Chocolate Strawberry Smoothie

Ingredients:

- 1 cup frozen strawberries
- 1 ripe banana
- 1 cup milk (dairy or plant-based)
- 2 tablespoons cocoa powder
- 1-2 tablespoons honey or maple syrup (adjust to taste)
- Ice cubes (optional, for a colder smoothie)
- Optional add-ins: a handful of spinach or kale, a scoop of protein powder, a tablespoon of chia seeds or flaxseeds

Instructions:

1. In a blender, combine the frozen strawberries, banana, milk, cocoa powder, and honey or maple syrup.
2. If desired, add any optional add-ins such as spinach or kale, protein powder, or seeds.
3. Blend the ingredients on high speed until smooth and creamy.
4. Taste the smoothie and adjust the sweetness if needed by adding more honey or maple syrup.
5. If you prefer a colder smoothie, add a handful of ice cubes and blend again until smooth.
6. Once blended to your desired consistency, pour the chocolate strawberry smoothie into glasses.
7. Serve immediately and enjoy the delicious combination of chocolate and strawberries!

Chocolate Cherry Smoothie

Ingredients:

- 1 cup frozen cherries
- 1 ripe banana
- 1 cup milk (dairy or plant-based)
- 2 tablespoons cocoa powder
- 1-2 tablespoons honey or maple syrup (adjust to taste)
- Ice cubes (optional, for a colder smoothie)
- Optional add-ins: a handful of spinach or kale, a scoop of protein powder, a tablespoon of chia seeds or flaxseeds

Instructions:

1. In a blender, combine the frozen cherries, banana, milk, cocoa powder, and honey or maple syrup.
2. If desired, add any optional add-ins such as spinach or kale, protein powder, or seeds.
3. Blend the ingredients on high speed until smooth and creamy.
4. Taste the smoothie and adjust the sweetness if needed by adding more honey or maple syrup.
5. If you prefer a colder smoothie, add a handful of ice cubes and blend again until smooth.
6. Once blended to your desired consistency, pour the chocolate cherry smoothie into glasses.
7. Serve immediately and enjoy the delicious combination of chocolate and cherries!

Chocolate Almond Smoothie

Ingredients:

- 1 ripe banana
- 1 cup almond milk (or any milk of your choice)
- 2 tablespoons cocoa powder
- 2 tablespoons almond butter
- 1-2 tablespoons honey or maple syrup (adjust to taste)
- 1/2 teaspoon vanilla extract
- Ice cubes (optional, for a colder smoothie)
- Optional add-ins: a handful of spinach or kale, a scoop of protein powder, a tablespoon of chia seeds or flaxseeds

Instructions:

1. In a blender, combine the ripe banana, almond milk, cocoa powder, almond butter, honey or maple syrup, and vanilla extract.
2. If desired, add any optional add-ins such as spinach or kale, protein powder, or seeds.
3. Blend the ingredients on high speed until smooth and creamy.
4. Taste the smoothie and adjust the sweetness if needed by adding more honey or maple syrup.
5. If you prefer a colder smoothie, add a handful of ice cubes and blend again until smooth.
6. Once blended to your desired consistency, pour the chocolate almond smoothie into glasses.
7. Serve immediately and enjoy the creamy and nutty flavor of this delicious smoothie!

Chocolate Oatmeal Smoothie

Ingredients:

- 1 ripe banana
- 1/2 cup rolled oats
- 1 cup milk (dairy or plant-based)
- 2 tablespoons cocoa powder
- 1 tablespoon honey or maple syrup (adjust to taste)
- 1/2 teaspoon vanilla extract
- Ice cubes (optional, for a colder smoothie)
- Optional add-ins: a handful of spinach or kale, a scoop of protein powder, a tablespoon of chia seeds or flaxseeds

Instructions:

1. In a blender, combine the ripe banana, rolled oats, milk, cocoa powder, honey or maple syrup, and vanilla extract.
2. If desired, add any optional add-ins such as spinach or kale, protein powder, or seeds.
3. Blend the ingredients on high speed until smooth and creamy.
4. Taste the smoothie and adjust the sweetness if needed by adding more honey or maple syrup.
5. If you prefer a thicker smoothie, you can let it sit for a few minutes to allow the oats to soften and thicken the mixture.
6. If you prefer a colder smoothie, add a handful of ice cubes and blend again until smooth.
7. Once blended to your desired consistency, pour the chocolate oatmeal smoothie into glasses.
8. Serve immediately and enjoy the nutritious and satisfying goodness of this chocolate oatmeal smoothie!

Chocolate Chia Seed Pudding

Ingredients:

- 1/4 cup chia seeds
- 1 cup milk (dairy or plant-based)
- 2 tablespoons cocoa powder
- 1-2 tablespoons honey or maple syrup (adjust to taste)
- 1/2 teaspoon vanilla extract
- Optional toppings: sliced bananas, berries, nuts, shredded coconut, chocolate chips

Instructions:

1. In a bowl or jar, combine the chia seeds, milk, cocoa powder, honey or maple syrup, and vanilla extract.
2. Stir the ingredients together until well combined.
3. Cover the bowl or jar and refrigerate the mixture for at least 4 hours or overnight, allowing the chia seeds to absorb the liquid and thicken into pudding-like consistency.
4. After chilling, give the pudding a good stir to redistribute the chia seeds.
5. Taste the pudding and adjust the sweetness if needed by adding more honey or maple syrup.
6. Serve the chocolate chia seed pudding in individual bowls or jars, and top with your favorite toppings such as sliced bananas, berries, nuts, shredded coconut, or chocolate chips.
7. Enjoy the rich and creamy chocolate chia seed pudding as a satisfying and nutritious dessert or snack!

Chocolate Banana Milkshake

Ingredients:

- 2 ripe bananas
- 2 cups milk (dairy or plant-based)
- 2 tablespoons cocoa powder
- 2 tablespoons honey or maple syrup (adjust to taste)
- 1/2 teaspoon vanilla extract
- 2 cups ice cubes

Instructions:

1. Peel the ripe bananas and cut them into chunks.
2. In a blender, combine the banana chunks, milk, cocoa powder, honey or maple syrup, and vanilla extract.
3. Add the ice cubes to the blender.
4. Blend the ingredients on high speed until smooth and creamy.
5. Taste the milkshake and adjust the sweetness if needed by adding more honey or maple syrup.
6. If the milkshake is too thick, you can add more milk to reach your desired consistency.
7. Once blended to your liking, pour the chocolate banana milkshake into glasses.
8. Optionally, garnish with a sprinkle of cocoa powder or whipped cream on top.
9. Serve immediately and enjoy the delicious and refreshing chocolate banana milkshake!

Chocolate Orange Milkshake

Ingredients:

- 2 ripe bananas
- 1 cup orange juice (freshly squeezed or store-bought)
- 1/2 cup milk (dairy or plant-based)
- 2 tablespoons cocoa powder
- 2 tablespoons honey or maple syrup (adjust to taste)
- Zest of 1 orange (optional, for extra flavor)
- 1/2 teaspoon vanilla extract
- 2 cups ice cubes

Instructions:

1. Peel the ripe bananas and cut them into chunks.
2. In a blender, combine the banana chunks, orange juice, milk, cocoa powder, honey or maple syrup, orange zest (if using), and vanilla extract.
3. Add the ice cubes to the blender.
4. Blend the ingredients on high speed until smooth and creamy.
5. Taste the milkshake and adjust the sweetness if needed by adding more honey or maple syrup.
6. If the milkshake is too thick, you can add more orange juice or milk to reach your desired consistency.
7. Once blended to your liking, pour the chocolate orange milkshake into glasses.
8. Optionally, garnish with a slice of orange or a sprinkle of cocoa powder on top.
9. Serve immediately and enjoy the refreshing and citrusy flavor of this chocolate orange milkshake!

Chocolate Coffee Milkshake

Ingredients:

- 2 cups vanilla ice cream
- 1/2 cup cold brewed coffee (or 1-2 shots of espresso, cooled)
- 1/2 cup milk (dairy or plant-based)
- 2 tablespoons cocoa powder
- 2 tablespoons chocolate syrup
- 1-2 tablespoons sugar or sweetener, to taste
- Whipped cream, for topping (optional)
- Chocolate shavings or cocoa powder, for garnish (optional)

Instructions:

1. In a blender, combine the vanilla ice cream, cold brewed coffee (or espresso), milk, cocoa powder, chocolate syrup, and sugar or sweetener.
2. Blend on high speed until smooth and creamy.
3. Taste the milkshake and adjust sweetness or coffee flavor as needed, adding more sugar or coffee to your preference.
4. If the milkshake is too thick, you can add a little more milk and blend again until desired consistency is reached.
5. Once blended to your liking, pour the chocolate coffee milkshake into glasses.
6. Optionally, top with whipped cream and garnish with chocolate shavings or a sprinkle of cocoa powder.
7. Serve immediately and enjoy the rich and indulgent flavor of this chocolate coffee milkshake!

Chocolate Caramel Milkshake

Ingredients:

- 2 cups vanilla ice cream
- 1/2 cup milk (dairy or plant-based)
- 2 tablespoons cocoa powder
- 2 tablespoons caramel sauce, plus extra for drizzling
- 1-2 tablespoons sugar or sweetener, to taste
- Whipped cream, for topping (optional)
- Chocolate shavings or cocoa powder, for garnish (optional)

Instructions:

1. In a blender, combine the vanilla ice cream, milk, cocoa powder, caramel sauce, and sugar or sweetener.
2. Blend on high speed until smooth and creamy.
3. Taste the milkshake and adjust sweetness as needed, adding more sugar if desired.
4. If the milkshake is too thick, you can add a little more milk and blend again until desired consistency is reached.
5. Once blended to your liking, drizzle caramel sauce around the inside of the glasses.
6. Pour the chocolate caramel milkshake into the glasses.
7. Optionally, top with whipped cream and garnish with chocolate shavings or a sprinkle of cocoa powder.
8. Serve immediately and enjoy the decadent flavor of this chocolate caramel milkshake!

Chocolate Hazelnut Milkshake

Ingredients:

- 2 cups vanilla ice cream
- 1/2 cup milk (dairy or plant-based)
- 2 tablespoons cocoa powder
- 2 tablespoons chocolate hazelnut spread (such as Nutella)
- 1-2 tablespoons sugar or sweetener, to taste
- Whipped cream, for topping (optional)
- Crushed hazelnuts or chocolate shavings, for garnish (optional)

Instructions:

1. In a blender, combine the vanilla ice cream, milk, cocoa powder, chocolate hazelnut spread, and sugar or sweetener.
2. Blend on high speed until smooth and creamy.
3. Taste the milkshake and adjust sweetness as needed, adding more sugar if desired.
4. If the milkshake is too thick, you can add a little more milk and blend again until desired consistency is reached.
5. Once blended to your liking, pour the chocolate hazelnut milkshake into glasses.
6. Optionally, top with whipped cream and garnish with crushed hazelnuts or chocolate shavings.
7. Serve immediately and enjoy the rich and indulgent flavor of this chocolate hazelnut milkshake!

Chocolate Mint Milkshake

Ingredients:

- 2 cups vanilla ice cream
- 1/2 cup milk (dairy or plant-based)
- 2 tablespoons cocoa powder
- 1/2 teaspoon peppermint extract
- 1-2 tablespoons sugar or sweetener, to taste
- Green food coloring (optional)
- Whipped cream, for topping (optional)
- Chocolate shavings or cocoa powder, for garnish (optional)

Instructions:

1. In a blender, combine the vanilla ice cream, milk, cocoa powder, peppermint extract, and sugar or sweetener.
2. Add a few drops of green food coloring if desired, for a more vibrant mint color.
3. Blend on high speed until smooth and creamy.
4. Taste the milkshake and adjust sweetness as needed, adding more sugar if desired.
5. If the milkshake is too thick, you can add a little more milk and blend again until desired consistency is reached.
6. Once blended to your liking, pour the chocolate mint milkshake into glasses.
7. Optionally, top with whipped cream and garnish with chocolate shavings or a sprinkle of cocoa powder.
8. Serve immediately and enjoy the refreshing and minty flavor of this chocolate mint milkshake!

Chocolate Coconut Milkshake

Ingredients:

- 2 cups vanilla ice cream
- 1/2 cup coconut milk (canned or carton)
- 2 tablespoons cocoa powder
- 2 tablespoons shredded coconut (sweetened or unsweetened)
- 1-2 tablespoons sugar or sweetener, to taste
- Whipped cream, for topping (optional)
- Toasted coconut flakes, for garnish (optional)

Instructions:

1. In a blender, combine the vanilla ice cream, coconut milk, cocoa powder, shredded coconut, and sugar or sweetener.
2. Blend on high speed until smooth and creamy.
3. Taste the milkshake and adjust sweetness as needed, adding more sugar if desired.
4. If the milkshake is too thick, you can add a little more coconut milk and blend again until desired consistency is reached.
5. Once blended to your liking, pour the chocolate coconut milkshake into glasses.
6. Optionally, top with whipped cream and garnish with toasted coconut flakes.
7. Serve immediately and enjoy the tropical and chocolaty flavor of this chocolate coconut milkshake!

Chocolate Berry Milkshake

Ingredients:

- 2 cups vanilla ice cream
- 1/2 cup milk (dairy or plant-based)
- 2 tablespoons cocoa powder
- 1 cup mixed berries (such as strawberries, raspberries, and blueberries)
- 1-2 tablespoons sugar or sweetener, to taste
- Whipped cream, for topping (optional)
- Fresh berries, for garnish (optional)

Instructions:

1. In a blender, combine the vanilla ice cream, milk, cocoa powder, mixed berries, and sugar or sweetener.
2. Blend on high speed until smooth and creamy.
3. Taste the milkshake and adjust sweetness as needed, adding more sugar if desired.
4. If the milkshake is too thick, you can add a little more milk and blend again until desired consistency is reached.
5. Once blended to your liking, pour the chocolate berry milkshake into glasses.
6. Optionally, top with whipped cream and garnish with fresh berries.
7. Serve immediately and enjoy the delicious combination of chocolate and berries in this milkshake!

Chocolate Vanilla Milkshake

Ingredients:

- 2 cups vanilla ice cream
- 1/2 cup milk (dairy or plant-based)
- 2 tablespoons cocoa powder
- 1-2 tablespoons sugar or sweetener, to taste
- 1 teaspoon vanilla extract
- Whipped cream, for topping (optional)
- Chocolate shavings or cocoa powder, for garnish (optional)

Instructions:

1. In a blender, combine the vanilla ice cream, milk, cocoa powder, sugar or sweetener, and vanilla extract.
2. Blend on high speed until smooth and creamy.
3. Taste the milkshake and adjust sweetness as needed, adding more sugar if desired.
4. If the milkshake is too thick, you can add a little more milk and blend again until desired consistency is reached.
5. Once blended to your liking, pour the chocolate vanilla milkshake into glasses.
6. Optionally, top with whipped cream and garnish with chocolate shavings or a sprinkle of cocoa powder.
7. Serve immediately and enjoy the classic flavor combination of chocolate and vanilla in this milkshake!

www.ingramcontent.com/pod-product-compliance
Lightning Source LLC
LaVergne TN
LVHW081333060526
838201LV00055B/2614